WHAT IS
TRUE RELIGION?

✘CULTIVATING BIBLICAL GODLINESS

Series Editors
Joel R. Beeke and Ryan M. McGraw

Dr. D. Martyn Lloyd-Jones once said that what the church needs to do most of all is "to begin herself to live the Christian life. If she did that, men and women would be crowding into our buildings. They would say, 'What is the secret of this?'" As Christians, one of our greatest needs is for the Spirit of God to cultivate biblical godliness in us in order to put the beauty of Christ on display through us, all to the glory of the triune God. With this goal in mind, this series of booklets treats matters vital to Christian experience at a basic level. Each booklet addresses a specific question in order to inform the mind, warm the affections, and transform the whole person by the Spirit's grace, so that the church may adorn the doctrine of God our Savior in all things.

WHAT IS
TRUE RELIGION?

GEOFFREY THOMAS

REFORMATION HERITAGE BOOKS
GRAND RAPIDS, MICHIGAN

Reformation Heritage Books
2965 Leonard St. NE
Grand Rapids, MI 49525
616-977-0889
orders@heritagebooks.org
www.heritagebooks.org

Printed in the United States of America
20 21 22 23 24 25/10 9 8 7 6 5 4 3 2 1

ISBN 978-1-60178-818-4
ISBN 978-1-60178-819-1 (e-pub)

For additional Reformed literature, request a free book list from Reformation Heritage Books at the above regular or e-mail address.

WHAT IS
TRUE RELIGION?

Is there a more important question to be answered than that? What a quest to take up, to think and to inquire about, and then to discover the ultimate reality of personally knowing the living God and being known by Him.

There are many religions, ancient and modern. Many vile and unspeakable acts have been done and are being done in the name of the world's religions. There is nothing particularly contemporary in the question, "What is true religion?" The Lord Jesus Christ was crucified in the name of religion almost 2,000 years ago, and this same question as to where reality in religion could be found was being asked in His day as it is in ours.

The Pharisees had been the most influential religious group in Israel at the time of Christ for at least two centuries, and if a Pharisee should have been asked the question as to the nature of real religion he might have answered it in at least three ways.

1. You had to believe in the God who had revealed Himself to the authors and prophets of the Old Testament, and that this God was the one true and living God, and that the entire Old Testament was His revelation, and that Israel were the one true people of God (see Rom. 2:17–29).

2. You had to follow the entirety of the laws given in the Old Testament. Among other things, this would have meant attendance at the synagogue on the Sabbath day and circumcision of your male sons. It meant fasting on certain days and ceremonially washing your hands and letting them dry naturally without a towel before eating a meal. It entailed going to Jerusalem three times a year and there at its temple offering the prescribed sacrifices. It also involved tithing, that is, giving a tenth of all you possessed to God, even of the herbs that were in your garden (see Matt. 6:2–4; 23:25–26; Mark 7:3–4; Phil. 3:5–6).

3. In addition, you had to remove certain things from your life. For example, you had to refuse to eat pork, venison, and lobster, rejecting them as unclean meats. You had to cease mixing with non-Pharisees, declining to visit their homes, to attend their weddings, or to accept an invitation to go to their parties. In fact, if you were truly zealous for God, you hated those you regarded as wicked. And you might even kill those you regarded as apostate from God (see Matt. 5:43; 23:29–32; Phil. 3:6).

So true religion for the Pharisee consisted of not only believing certain things, but also adding certain patterns of behavior to your life and also cutting out certain practices from your life.

Now today some of these are still the ways the majority of people believe they are showing that they've got real religion. When some Christian students at university were asked why more fellow students would not attend meetings of the Christian Union, a discerning young man replied thus: "They think of us as declaring that we are the self-appointed upholders of morality at college, that our whole message to the students consists of such exhortations as live a moral life, do not drink, do not take drugs, and do not have sex before marriage." Such actions and such abstinences are dismissed by the majority of students, and so they have no intention of attending religious meetings where such behavior is encouraged. They are not in the least sympathetic to a moralistic Christianity.

The Lord Jesus was a total enigma to the people of His day (Mark 4:41). He was by every criteria a holy man. He preached the Scriptures powerfully (Matt. 7:28–29). Mothers put their young children into His arms for Him to pray for them and bless them (Matt. 19:13–15). Christ even allowed a woman to sit before Him and weep, drying His tear-stained feet with her hair (Luke 7:37–38). But He took no illicit advantage of her devotion to Him. He made no money from His religion, having earned more as a village carpenter than as a rabbi who could draw large crowds to His seminars.

Yet our Lord did not define real religion as consisting of adding certain patterns of behavior to one's life or subtracting other practices. Nor did He teach His disciples that in focusing on such additions and subtractions they could discover life in all its fullness. When He explained to His hearers the nature of true religion, He told them that it consisted of a new relationship with God through Himself (John 17:3). This relationship consisted of such things as learning from Jesus's teaching, for all that He taught was from God (John 7:46). This relationship with God also consisted of worshiping the Lord Jesus as God (John 20:28; 1 John 5:20). It consisted of entrusting themselves to God's mercy through the sacrifice of Jesus Christ as the Lamb of God who made atonement for their sin by His dying on the cross (John 1:29). This relationship with Jehovah Jesus (John 8:58) consisted of His protection and care of them by His mighty power as one who has all authority in earth and even in heaven (Matt. 28:18–20). He claimed that it was not possible for anyone to come to God except by Him. He alone was, and is, the way (John 14:6). This was His constant theme, that through our entrusting ourselves to Him by grace as our teacher, and priest, and mighty sovereign protector that then God will be reconciled to us. Those are either the claims of a megalomaniac or they are the truths of the one true Creator and redeeming God who has spoken for centuries through Moses and the prophets, but now most clearly of all through His Son, Jesus Christ (Heb. 1:1–3).

The contrast between Himself and the Pharisees was salutary. "What is wrong with fasting?" they asked. "Why don't you teach it? It is in the Scriptures. You have been known to fast, and John the Baptist, whom you admire, fasted, and he taught his disciples to fast, but what do we see in you? That neither you nor they regularly fast, nor are you teaching the crowds that come to your meetings to fast. What's the matter with you?" (cf. Mark 2:18).

WHAT IS TRUE RELIGION?

The Lord Jesus answered their queries in a most arresting way. He asked them whether people going to a marriage service actually attend that happy occasion in order to mourn and fast there (Mark 2:19). Of course they do not. The service is joyful as well as serious. The wedding hymns praise the goodness of the God who has brought this man and woman into the holy and happy estate of matrimony. There is prayer for God's blessing on their futures as new husband and wife. There are photographs, and then there is often a feast, maybe a minor one of such delicacies as strawberries and cream and cake, and a major smaller gathering of the family, the bridal party, and close friends.

At that occasion, after thanks is said to God for the food, the waiters and waitresses come around with the first course. "Soup or melon?" they ask. But what if everyone at one table, who are friends of the groom, refuse everything, and the waiter notices that they are all dressed in black (a traditional color in Western societies for mourning attire), and weeping? Then, the second course comes around and the waiter brings to the table a steaming jug of gravy, a bowl of peas with a lump of butter on the top, a silver dish of roast potatoes, a platter of hot tender beef, a variety of vegetables, and so on. But what if all the guests at that one table shake their heads and say quietly, "Nothing for us, thank you." Would not the bride's father be furious at the shadow that this melancholy is casting over the whole occasion? Would he not turn to his new son-in-law and ask him what's wrong with his friends? He urges him to talk to them. They have not come to bury him but to celebrate this life-changing happy event in his life. "Encourage them to enter into the spirit of the occasion and enjoy this good food. I have spent a lot of money on this feast," he adds. But the groom's exhortations are ignored. There is a stand-off and a grim tense depression settles on the wedding feast. The news of the strange behavior at the wedding leaks out. The press gets hold of it. Reuters send it around the world, "The Wedding That Was Turned into a Wake." What a lot of cranks! And the world mocks.

There are times for true fasting that reflect a grief-filled heart. After the crucifixion of Christ, two of His disciples, Cleopas and a friend, were walking to Emmaus in the deepest sadness, with no appetite for food (Luke 24:14–15). Their beloved teacher and friend had been wrenched away from them by wicked men and nailed to a cross, was dead and buried. When He was with them what hope and joy they had known, but not now. They thought they would never get over this, the worst of all possible calamities that they'd ever known or ever would experience. There is a time for grief and fasting, but that time is not a wedding day when the groom and his bride are full of excitement and delight.

Real religion is characterized by a wellspring of joy springing up in our hearts at the discovery of the living Son of God who loves us, forgives our sins, gives us genuine peace, and shares our burdens by yoking Himself to us to help us carry our load (1 Peter 1:8; Matt. 11:30). He is there at our side day after day, never ceasing in His loving care, always telling us what the truth is, explaining why mankind is in the state it is in, and how the world can know redemption and mercy so that sinners who now have come to believe in Jesus can have illimitable access to an indwelling Savior. What are these new feelings of blessedness and joy? They are quite impossible to put into words. The living, resurrected Jesus Christ has come and dealt with our ignorance by teaching us what is true. He has dealt with our guilt and shame by Himself choosing to take our condemnation which He experienced while hanging in the darkness on the cross under God's judgment (Isa. 53:6). He has dealt with our weakness by His powerful presence in us, around us, alongside us, before us, beneath us, above us, and behind us, promising He will never, never leave us. These realities banish a gloomy spirit. Our beloved Bridegroom is always with us, Jesus the lover of our souls! We are experiencing the delight of a first love that never becomes stale. So, this Christian life is not to be characterized by mourning and fasting. We can rejoice in the Lord always (Phil. 4:4). Every day we bless him. Jesus Christ tells us what true religion is: it is focused on receiving Him into our lives as our loving Lord and Savior.

In fact, He is the one who enables us to receive Him and He also sustains that relationship throughout our entire lives. The Christian life is much more than ethical additions to and moral subtractions of sin from our lives. The moral changes and the transformation of our affections are certainly there in all true religion, but they are the consequences of being gripped by true religion and that consists of embracing a lifelong Christ-centered and Christ-dependent attitude and lifestyle as you say, "For to me to live is Christ" (Phil. 1:21).

TAKE CARE WHAT YOU ADD TO YOUR LIFE

The Lord Jesus also used another familiar image to explain the nature of true religion. He once said that no wife or mother ever did a good job of patching the clothes of her family if she sewed pieces of brand-new unwashed cloth onto a worn-out garment. As a boy, Jesus in Nazareth had possibly watched His mother over the years patching His own clothes as well as those of His half brothers and half sisters. When a garment was beyond repair, she might have kept it in a garment drawer, bringing it out when a similar garment of the same color needed patching usually at the knees or the bottom. She would cut from the unworn sides of those old garments a patch and sew it onto these worn clothes. She would never use new cloth because there was no preshrunk new garments in those days. If she attached a patch of new cloth to an old garment then at the first wash that material could shrink to half its size. Then the threadbare part would be torn into two rendering it virtually unrepairable. Old garments must have old patches attached to them (Matt. 9:16).

The Lord is warning us that we can add unsuitable things to our lives. A bad situation could be made much worse by the action of adding the wrong things to your life. For example, a married couple are going through difficult months in their marriage and so they go to a man who claims to be a marriage counselor. They explain their tensions and fights to him; finally he makes suggestions about what they might do to spice up their marriage. He suggests certain behaviors which to them seem both abhorrent and shocking. And when they later attempt to act in those ways, they are repulsed and find themselves even further apart from one another than they had been before. Take care what you add to your life, Jesus is warning His followers.

Or there are parents concerned about the behavior of a teenage son. He is staying out late, mixing with a gang of good-for-nothings, and watching questionable programs on the web. There are certain odors that hang around him when he returns home late and they suspect he has started using drugs, which he denies. He brushes aside angrily their concerns and finally they go to see a counselor in his school. "Don't worry!" is the counselor's advice. "This is just a phase that all boys go through. Just ignore it. He will grow out of it. Don't antagonize him." They take this advice but have a deepening concern for their son's behavior that is confirmed one day when the doorbell rings and there, outside the house, are two policemen. Their boy is in serious trouble and since they added the wrong counsel to their life as a family, they have failed to help him. They have added to the situation a new detachment when the old way of loving discipline, care, prayer, and tearful entreaty was the way to go. They added a detachment and silence that made a bad situation worse.

If you are adding something to your life you must make sure that it is old cloth strengthening an old garment. It is often said that if something is true it is not new, and if it is new it is not true. What are we referring to? Look around you at the glorious creation. It speaks to us each day of its Creator (Ps. 19:1). It declares to us that the infinite and almighty God who made all this by a word in the beginning is transcendentally glorious (Rom. 1:20). How mighty He is, the Ancient of days (Dan. 7:9–10). Our worship must be commensurate with the glory of His holiness, justice, and truth.

Or let's consider your conscience. That is the great monitor that God has set in every human being, and it rebukes us when we do wrong and commends us when we do right. How old is your conscience? "How old?" You say that your conscience is as old as you are. You have always had a conscience. Then do you heed that voice? To the person who knows what is good but refuses to do it then for that person his behavior is sinful behavior. Always let your conscience be your guide, especially if it is a conscience enlightened by an earlier grace. The French reformer John Calvin once said, "The torture of a bad conscience is the hell of a living soul." The creation's voice is old cloth. Your conscience can also be old cloth to start patching up your threadbare life.

Or again there is the old cloth of the message of the Bible. You find lives wrapped in it everywhere in the world today, from Wall Street in New York to those living in some of the vast slums of Nairobi, Kenya. You also find millions newly clothed in this message in China and even in Afghanistan. All kinds and classes of men and women are embraced by it. The banker and the beggar put their trust in this good news. It is believed by the elderly and by children, scientists and farmers, the wealthy and the impoverished. There are more Christians in the world today than ever before. It is no ghetto group living merely in one part of the globe. The good news of Jesus Christ encircles the world. It is truly a global faith.

Four thousand years ago, there was a man named Abram (later called Abraham), who lived in Ur, a town at the heart of the civilized world. God came and spoke to him, telling him to move and go to a place that he had prepared for the patriarch (Gen. 12:1). Abram heard the word of God and he acted upon it, and so became the model and the father of all who have experienced the true faith ever since, as he had done (Heb. 11:8–19). The same God speaks to us in the message of the Bible today. For example, "God so loved the world, that he gave his only begotten Son, that whosoever believeth in him should not perish, but have everlasting life" (John 3:16). We deserve eternal death for the way we have pushed God out of our lives. He is in none of our thoughts (Ps. 10:4), but this neglected Lord, Jesus Christ, God the Son, because He loved us, still came and He lived for us and with us. He shed His blood to make atonement for our sins because God is merciful and good. The Son of God died in our place bearing the judgment we deserve (Gal. 3:13), and we are forgiven for all our sins through what the Lord did—all by Himself, and in such a demonstration of the wonderful love of God for careless, bored, and indifferent people like ourselves (1 John 3:16–18). If you have a rather threadbare religion, then you need to find this old cloth to patch it up and strengthen your life. In the old message of the gospel, you will find that good cloth that delivers us from many embarrassments and shame. We are not sighing and wringing our hands looking for something that can effectively patch up our lives. God is offering to us this superstrong and enduring cloth that He has created and that He provides for us. It was woven in Bethlehem, and Nazareth, Galilee, and at the cross on Golgotha. It is most suitable for everyone who longs for it. It can cover all our shameful and threadbare morality.

SOMETHING MORE IS NEEDED THAN A PATCHED-UP LIFE

Another image is used by the Lord Jesus. God is not warning us about doing certain wrong actions and exhorting us to introduce new practices into our lives. Rather, what He is doing is this: He is offering us the most delicious wine from heaven (Joel 3:18). He is offering us the life of eternity and this life is characterized by the fruitful Spirit of love, joy, peace, longsuffering, gentleness, goodness, faith, meekness, and temperance (Gal. 5:22–23). Those are the flavors of a heaven-made wine. Listen to the Bible's description of its aroma. It is characterized by making those who imbibe it turn from their cocky and bombastic ways to become poor in spirit. They no longer pamper their egos but mourn over their shortcomings, they become meek and humble, and long for a more righteous way of life. They seek to become pure in heart and peacemakers. They are prepared to suffer for the truth without compromising their new convictions (Matt. 5:2–12). What a delightful aroma has this divine wine of heaven! Its bouquet strengthens those who have received it as indispensable for their cross-bearing and self-denial. That is the medicinal joy-creating wine of the Spirit of God that is freely given to all of God's repenting, believing people. They can say, "I rejoiced in the Lord and afterward I knew that He had come into my life and caused my heart to leap for joy."

So true religion demands that we ourselves have to be changed if we are to receive and know the transforming influence of such pure and powerful heavenly wine. The Lord Jesus once said, "No man putteth new wine into old bottles: else the new wine doth burst the bottles, and the wine is spilled, and the bottles will be marred: but new wine must be put into new bottles" (Mark 2:22). At the time of Christ, when a sheep was slaughtered the skin was carefully removed. There were six orifices. The five apertures for the legs and the anus were carefully bound up and a nozzle—a hollow bone—was attached to where the head had been. The skin was then carefully cured. New wine expands and if it is in a new wineskin that skin possesses a pliability. It will expand with the wine until the fermentation process is complete. The older a wineskin is the more brittle it becomes. It is fine as a water container for a traveler, but useless for holding new wine.

The Lord Jesus is opening up this theme of explaining the nature of true religion and He is telling us again that real religion entails far more than adding resolutions and moral changes to your life. You yourself need to change. You need a new heart (Ezek. 18:31). You have to be made by God into a new creation (2 Cor. 5:17). You must be born again (John 3:3). All things in your life need to be renewed. Adding religious behavior is simply not enough.

Consider a teenager who feels guilty about his life and thinks he will add church attendance to "make himself better." By no means would I want to depreciate going to church, and experiencing the remarkable influence that other Christians you meet can have over you. We need to belong to the people of God, for the Holy Spirit unites every Christian to every other believer, thus making us one in the Spirit (1 Cor. 12:13; Eph. 4:4). But mere attendance at any church can become an unfruitful experience in our quest to know what true religion is. It can be a mere routine, an alternative to an empty house. It is just another addendum to our lives if we do not hear the truth of the Bible in its warnings and promises applied to us.

Consider again a husband and wife who are having marital tensions. They read in a weekly magazine that couples who go to church have longer marriages and less divorces than those who never attend church. I believe that that is true. So, off they go to some church or other and listen to a religious message. But there is no guarantee that that addition is going to help them to discover what is the true faith. They have simply added some religious activity to their lives.

Or again consider a home where being a good neighbor is held in high esteem. It would be excellent if we were all good neighbors and helped in every way the folk who live near us, caring for their cat for a day or two when they are called away, watering their plants for a week when they are on vacation, keeping an eye on their home when they are visiting their families, and taking in their deliveries. Some who have discovered the nature of true religion will bear testimony to the folks next door, saying about them, "I have the best neighbors in the world. They are wonderful," and then they will add, "but they have no interest in Jesus Christ at all." They simply believe that it is important to be good neighbors. They will not attend church and are not prepared to talk about the Bible.

Or once again there are wonderfully generous people whom we meet. How kindhearted they are, self-sacrificial, remembering birthdays and weddings and anniversaries. They will bring a cake on some special day. They will drive you to an appointment if your car is broken down. "We are here to support one another," they say, but they have no desire to know and love God. They always have a reason why they cannot come to some special church service. They are people who have added some works of thoughtfulness to their lives maybe because of an earlier grace in their families or in the land. But in their hearts there is no affection for the dearest and loveliest Man that this world has ever seen.

Let me use this illustration. A man loves his garden, but groans at the crab apple tree that is prominently situated right at the heart of the greenery. He can do nothing with its apples. They are as small and hard as ball bearings and as bitter as lemons, setting your teeth on edge. One day he has an idea. He buys a bag of delicious apples—good for both baking and eating—and soon afterwards he goes out with scissors and string and ties each one onto the crab apple tree. He takes a shower and then goes back to his favorite chair and gazes at the new presence in the garden. There stands the tree covered with these delicious apples shining in the sun. What a sight! How happy he feels. But what actually is that tree? It is a crab apple tree still, with some temporary additions attached to it. It has not changed in itself organically. It has simply had a temporary cosmetic change of appearance (Matt. 12:33).

Again, consider a teenager who passes his driving exam and proceeds to purchase an old car. He sprays it yellow. He adds artificial zebra-skin seat covers. He puts in an audio system so that you can hear him coming from a block away, and so on. The vehicle is his pride and joy, but what is it? A souped-up old clunker of a car. That is what it will always be. Do you see that real religion is not attained by adding moral patterns of behavior to your life? It is not attained by adding good religious actions to your life, like fasting and saying your prayers and going to church regularly. You yourself are the one who needs to be changed from within.

A little girl was looking at a bowl of flowers and one or two of them were just in bud. So, she picked one out of the pot and peeled back the green outward covering and began to open up the tight bud of blossom. Ten minutes later when her mother entered the room she found her in tears. "What's wrong?" she asked. "I have destroyed this flower," she said pointing to the bud she has torn apart lying in pieces on the table. "I was only trying to help," she mourned. Her mother comforted her. "Do you see, darling, that the flower has to open from the inside?" And so it is with us. We have to change from within. We have to be made new wineskins if we are going to be changed by imbibing the powerful, life-changing, delightful wine of heaven.

WHY IS SUCH A FUNDAMENTAL ERROR MADE?

Why do people make such a fundamental mistake? What is their error? They do not understand the problem that all humanity is facing. They are thinking that men and women are under the disapproval of God because of their sins. They worship idols, they ignore the Lord's Day, they blaspheme, they are violent, they commit sexual sin, they steal, and they covet what belongs to others. Those are the reasons why God is angry with them, they think.

A wife loves her husband and she might say, "If only he could stop swearing, he would be a perfect man." What is the fundamental error we men and women are making when we think and speak like that? It is this error, that we are not under condemnation because of our sins. We are condemned because we are sinners. We are by nature the children of wrath, that is, God's wrath from heaven hones in on us because of the state of our hearts, which are deceitful and desperately wicked in His sight. Our hearts are at enmity against God. We are refusing to allow Jesus Christ the Son of God to rule over us. We are living rebel lives.

We are under condemnation because of the rebellious indifference to God that dominates our natural hearts. Why does a child have measles? Is it because of the measles spots? No. It has the spots because it has the measles virus. There is no point in getting a cosmetic coloring to match the color of the child's skin and then camouflage every spot. That would do more harm than good. Why is a man ill? Because he has a high temperature? No. He has a high temperature because he is ill. He has a virus or some bacteria and then it is a course of antibiotics that will help to heal him.

The main problem in our nation today is not with the structures of society, as politicians, media people, writers, and religious leaders think. The

Victorian author Charles Dickens described in his great novels the problems in the factories, and in the pits, and in the law, and in the church, and in politics, and in education. All of them were structural problems that needed legislation to change them. Today there is violence, knife and gun crime, sexually transmitted diseases, the availability of the most explicit pornography, prisons packed to overflowing, access to drugs everywhere, abortions, addiction to alcohol, and gambling on an unprecedented scale. What enormous problems the Western world faces, and our society seems to be crumbling under the weight of all of these antisocial ways of life.

But these are all symptoms of sick individuals who function without any reference to the God in whom we all live and move and have our being. What is the disease that produces these symptoms? It is human sinfulness. There can be no understanding of what is true religion unless you accept the diagnosis insisted upon by real Christianity. The most important conviction you can have is the conviction of sin.

King David wrote in Psalm 23:1, "The LORD is my shepherd; I shall not want." With those words he clearly professes to be someone who has found true religion. But that religious king got trapped into infatuation for a married woman. He sent for her and they had an affair so that she became pregnant. He sent for her husband, requiring him to return to Jerusalem from the battle front hoping that he would go home and spend the night with his wife so that the child might appear to be his. The brave young soldier would not go home to his wife during a war in which his friends were risking their lives to serve king and country. He remained in the barracks. So, David arranged for him to be murdered. Could such a wretched evil act possibly come from someone who has true religion? The husband's fellow soldiers, during a skirmish, abandoned him to the enemy who killed him. Such was the way the much-married David got another wife. How shameful and how tragic!

For a year he masqueraded as the righteous husband of Bathsheba until God sent one of His prophets named Nathan to break David's cruel and deceitful heart. Nathan told David a story in which a man acted selfishly and unjustly, and when David professed anger at the man, the prophet turned on David and boldly told him, "Thou art the man" (2 Sam. 12:7). The king fell before Jehovah confessing his sins. David kept nothing back. He made no excuses for the evil of his conduct. He didn't apportion the blame to Bathsheba, accusing her of immodesty. He didn't plead that he was simply doing what all monarchs did with their power. He didn't plead that he was simply a more sexual man than others and that ought to be brought into consideration. None of those excuses were pleaded. What did King David say as he humbled himself in deep repentance before God? "For I acknowledge my transgressions: and my sin is ever before me. Against thee, thee only, have I sinned, and done this evil in thy sight: that thou mightest be justified when thou speakest, and be clear when thou judgest. Behold, I was shapen in iniquity; and in sin did my mother conceive me…. Deliver me from bloodguiltiness, O God, thou God of my salvation" (Ps. 51:3–5, 14). Those who possess true religion are not characterized by sinless and perfect lives, but they all are characterized by a repentance when they fall into sin that is commensurate with some awareness of the depth of the iniquity of their actions.

David's sin reveals that a person who possesses true religion is not a person without sin. But such a person will always acknowledge his sin and his need of mercy. He does not do so in some self-defensive way, saying, "Yes, I'm a sinner, but I am not like those people who go to church with their high and mighty ways. I am a simple sinner. I acknowledge it. There is nobody perfect." No! None of those self-accusing and self-pitying words of half-hearted "confession." Rather, the sigh and the tear, "What a depraved man I am!" You feel as evil as any of those who had true religion whose imperfect lives are recorded in the Bible. You sin as did Adam, and Noah, and Abraham, and Lot, and Moses, and Gideon, and Isaiah, and Peter, and Paul. You also stand in the solidarity of sinful fallenness with them and with all men, including those who possess true religion and you all confess humbly your sin and need of mercy day by day.

Have you seen that you need to change and must change and that God can change you? You will never desire a God-honoring, Christ-centered, truly happy life unless your own desires and longings are changed by God. In *The Times* newspaper on September 13, 2019, the readers were informed that Kentucky Fried Chicken had attempted to introduce some baked chicken products that were considered by many to be healthier food. They spent twelve million dollars installing ovens in order to sell baked or grilled chicken, but then they ran into customer rejection. Men and women refused to buy them. The "Brazer grilled chicken sandwich" was launched in 2011, the "Rancher sandwich" in 2012 and "Pulled Chicken" in 2015. All flopped and were dropped. If you launch a product that looks and tastes good and is also a healthy alternative, then, unless the customer buys and eats it, it is going to stay in the shop. KFC also decided to adapt its french fries making them healthier by cutting them slightly thicker. This resulted in cutting the calorie content by 18% and cutting fat by 12%, but once again customers refused to buy them. Customers had no intention of going to KFC in order to eat healthier food. To buy baked chicken, their own personal tastes and desires had to be changed.

So it is for you too in the metamorphosis that occurs when God enters your life. You will never know the blessedness of having the living God unless He makes you willing to want this by sweetly and powerfully working that longing into your heart and life. Jesus said that no one could come to Him unless God worked in a person's life, drawing him to Himself (John 6:44). So, will you start speaking to God and telling Him that your own heart and life are so cold that you still refuse to let Him into your life and that you will go on being as unchangeable as a marble statue until God makes such a dead object live?

Have you seen this? Have you felt the pain of your impotence? Have you said to God from your heart, "Have mercy upon me, O God, according to thy lovingkindness: according unto the multitude of thy tender mercies blot out my transgressions" (Ps. 51:1)? A stranger to personal acknowledgment of helplessness and sin is a stranger to true religion. There can be no real religious experience that bypasses confessing, "Helpless I come to Thee, "confessing our sins to God, and pleading for His mercy. Those who rejoice at the presence of the Bridegroom from heaven as their own Shepherd and Friend have arrived at that joy via a new realization of their helplessness, and a new mourning that they had lived too long without Him.

What is true religion? It is an attitude to God focused on His Son, the Lord Jesus Christ, who was sent by the living God after He had made Himself known to us through His servants the prophets.

Now He has come very close, adding forever to His divine nature real humanity, which was born of the virgin Mary, bone of our bones and flesh of our flesh. He lived the perfect life that no one else has been able to live, and that He did to fulfill all the righteousness that God requires of us all. He died to make atonement as the Lamb of God, propitiating the righteous anger of God at all that is cruel and hateful and despicable in us. He is our righteousness (2 Cor. 5:21), there exalted in heaven at the right hand of God the Father.

The Lord Jesus took that guilt and blame in the sacrifice of Himself on the cross. Behold the Lamb of God who takes away the sin of the world (John 1:29)! Peace with a holy sin-hating God through what Jesus Christ has done, and also is still doing as He lives and prays for us in heaven, and will yet do in the great day of resurrection that lies before us all.

That is true religion, reconciling a holy God to us sinful people through the loving work of His Son Jesus Christ our substitute. It is not adding some good religious behavior to our lives, like that man who tied a gross of apples onto a crab apple tree which completely failed to change the tree itself. Nor does true religion consist of attempting to remove every bad deed and word and thought from your life so that you can be fit to be saved. We are not saved by our good works, but we are saved for a new life of loving service (Eph. 2:8–10).

A man from Caerffili in Wales once told me that one morning he had gone out with his baby, taking the child to the local park. It was a cold February day, but the park was a beautiful winter scene. Then he noticed a strange sight. There was a grove of a dozen almost identical trees, apart from the fact that one of them was covered in dead leaves. The other eleven were all leafless. He wondered what the explanation for this might be and he came across the head gardener. "The park looks beautiful," he said. "You have done such a good job here. Just one thing puzzles me. That group of trees look all the same age and they are the same species, but one tree is covered in dead leaves. Do you know why?" The gardener nodded. "That tree with its leaves is a dead tree. It was struck by lightning last August."

There is a biological process called abscission whereby in the autumn a tree sheds its leaves. One of the reasons for this is that a heavy snowfall covering deciduous trees that had kept all their leaves could result in the possibility of branches being broken. So leaves are shed at the onset of winter. A living deciduous tree has no leaves in February. It is a parable of the Christian who at the favored time of receiving new life sheds such dead leaves as unbelief, and enmity against God, and defiance of the lordship of Jesus Christ, and prayerlessness. He does not do this in order to become alive to God. The new life of God that comes to him by the indwelling of the Spirit of Christ cuts those sins out of his life and this is what happens to every single Christian who becomes an adherent of true religion. These absences are the marks of saving faith in Christ.

Let us imagine what would happen if the head gardener on the next morning gathered the gardening boys around him to give them their instructions for the day. He says to them, "The time has come for us to do something about that dead sycamore tree with all it dark brown leaves. I am weary of people coming to me and asking why it still is covered in dead leaves. Get the ladders and I will give you the shears and pruning scissors and I want you to cut all those dead leaves off that tree. Start at the bottom and work your way up. You will do it by this afternoon." How the boys would complain, but they had to obey orders, and when he went to inspect their work by 4 p.m. he was very pleased with their industry and they went home an hour earlier. Now that tree appears exactly the same as the other live trees that are leafless in February, but it was still a dead tree. The superficial marks of death had been removed from it. The tree had the appearance of life, but it was dead.

TRUE RELIGION IS EXPERIENCED IN A NEW BIRTH

You can tie eating apples on to a tree but still the tree is a crab apple tree. You can remove all the dead leaves from a dead tree in winter but that leafless tree is not alive. You have merely changed the appearance of both trees, but neither has changed in itself.

A man whose name was Nicodemus once came at night to talk to the Lord Christ (John 3:1–2). He had come to the conclusion that Jesus must have come to earth from God. That was the only explanation Nicodemus could see for the extraordinary power the Lord had over disease and demons and death and the creation itself. He had added belief about Jesus being a divine messenger to his own moral values and his knowledge of the Scriptures, but Nicodemus with all his additions and subtractions still totally lacked true religion. He needed to become a new wineskin, and Jesus quickly diagnosed this and said to him, "Verily, verily, I say unto thee, Except a man be born again, he cannot see the kingdom of God" (John 3:3). Nicodemus needed a radical change of heart, a metamorphosis that was as striking as the change in a newly born baby from its prior existence in its mother's womb to one of breathing air and sucking its mother's milk and seeing everything around it.

There is no greater change in all of life than that which is wrought by the new birth. Not even death changes us as radically as being born from above by the Holy Spirit. True religion is characterized by being declared righteous by God. Our sins are all pardoned—past sins, present sins, future sins. The righteousness of Christ is imputed to us so that we are holy in Jesus Christ. We are made new creations and all things are made new to us. We are adopted into the family of God and now have God our Father's protection, access to His presence at any time, and recognition as being one of His many children. We are united to Jesus Christ, joined to Him like a branch in a tree, receiving His life day by day. Our status is totally changed; we have a place in heaven reserved for us (1 Peter 1:4). That place is more secure than the position the angels and archangels enjoy in heaven. We are in fact glorified in Jesus Christ (Rom. 8:30).

True religion is a gift from God that has been purchased for every single Christian by the life and death and intercession of the Son of God, Jesus Christ. Receiving that gift as it is freely offered to all who will accept it is the way to obtain true religion. Then going on as one has begun looking to the perfection of Jesus, praying to Him, finding help each day in the smallest and greatest of difficulties that we (with all men and women) have to meet, learning that you are able to cope in everything that God permits to come into your life through the strength and wisdom that the Lord provides.

How can you reject such a great religion? I can hardly understand how a person can hear of the Lord Jesus, His beautiful life and His mighty accomplishments for all whom He loves, and yet respond by saying, "Yes, but...." Would you dare say that? "I agree with much you have written, but...." Today you have read what true religion is, how it has been defined and applied by Jesus Christ. It is being offered to you now as a gift from God. How can you shrug? How is it possible for you to say to yourself, "The jury is still out." What are you waiting for? Are you wanting more tingles and elevated feelings before you turn from your unbelief and entrust yourself now and forever to the Savior? Are you demanding that God must give you those experiences before you decide to receive the gift of Jesus Christ, the Son of God, and His salvation? You are in no position to bargain with God. Isn't the resurrection of Christ from the dead enough for you? The only way I can understand your indifference to Jesus is that you are like everyone else and love darkness rather than love the light of Christ.

Be different! Do not hesitate any longer. Do not wait until you feel more worthy or more inspired. Receive the gift of God. This reception comes in a movement of your mind and will to the inviting Savior as God applies the truth of what you have been reading to your present condition, where you are just now, what your needs are, and you simply start talking to Jesus Christ, just like that man Nicodemus went one night and talked to Him.

Dialogue with Jesus! Tell Him about your thoughts and needs and doubts. Tell Him of the mess your life has been in at times. Talk to Him about the people you have hurt and ask Him to help them to forgive you. Tell Him that you cannot face the future without Him, that you know that you must die and you want Him with you in the years before that certain event and especially when you walk through the valley of the shadow of death. Just talk to Him, and never stop. And when you are sure that He lives and is now your very own Savior and Lord, then ask Him to help you worship and serve Him, living a useful life of true religion that can help others, and that you grow in usefulness to Him and His people. And never stop seeking His help.